GLAMIS CASTLE

It gives me great pleasure to welcome you to Glamis Castle.

This ancient castle is my family home, as it has been home to all of my predecessors since 1372 when my ancestor Sir John Lyon was granted the Thanage of Glamis by King Robert II.

The Castle has been added to and altered through the centuries and continues to evolve to this day. It is an important part of British heritage and steeped in history.

I very much hope you enjoy your visit to Glamis, here in the heart of Angus.

Simon Patrick Bowes Lyon,
19th Earl of Strathmore and Kinghorne

GLAMIS CASTLE

From the moment you first see Glamis framed against the backdrop
of the Angus hills you know you are approaching a very special place.
Glamis does not disappoint. Reputedly the Castle where Macbeth brutally
murdered King Duncan in Shakespeare's play, it also has a softer past.

The Castle is perhaps best known as the childhood home of Her Majesty
Queen Elizabeth The Queen Mother. It is also the birthplace of her
daughter, Her Royal Highness The Princess Margaret.

'As you approach it strikes you with awe and admiration,

by the many turrets and guided balustrades at top;

you have a full prospect of the gardens each side,

cut out into glass plots and adorned with evergreens.'

Daniel Defoe (1660–1731).

*The castle in 1775
during the 9th Earl's
lifetime. Portrait by
Nathaniel Dance.
Watercolour by
Thomas Girtin
(1775 - 1802)*

Glamis Castle has been the ancestral seat of the Lyon family since 1372 when Sir John Lyon was granted the Thanage of Glamis by King Robert II – the first of the Stewart Kings. Four years later he married the King's daughter, Princess Joanna, since when the Castle has been visited by many members of the Scottish and British Royal Families.

Built on the site of a Royal hunting lodge, the pink sandstone L-shaped tower house was remodelled in the 17th century and the building you see today is very much that magnificent creation, although like all great buildings it continues to evolve and mature. It is not only what has passed at Glamis that is important and fascinating, but its present and future relevance to the area and beyond.

CONTENTS

THE MAIN ROOMS

THE DINING ROOM

Installed in the 1850s by a group of craftsmen from northern England, this piece of Victorian splendour has a superb plaster ceiling decorated with thistles of Scotland, roses of England and lions of the Lyon family. Magnificent wood panelling of the finest English oak abounds. The history of the family is told throughout: by the stained glass in the windows, carved wood on the panelling and with painted heraldic shields, examples of which are shown here.

The Glamis lion, above, was a golden wedding present to the 13th Earl and Countess from their 11 children in 1903. On the same occasion their grandchildren also presented them with the grandfather clock, now displayed in the room. The inscribed plaque within the clock, shown here, details the names of 'their loving grandchildren'; all 27 of them!

IN COMMEMORATION OF THE GOLDEN WEDDING OF
CLAUD & FRANCES, EARL & COUNTESS OF STRATHMORE AND KINGHORN
MICHAELMAS DAY 1903.
THIS CLOCK IS PRESENTED BY THEIR LOVING GRANDCHILDREN.

MARY	MURIEL				
PATRICK	CHARLES				
JOHN	GEOFFREY	HUBERT			
ALEXANDER	DORIS	JOAN	GAVIN	PHYLLIS	ALFRED
FERGUS	WINIFRED	EFFIE	ANGUS	LESLIE	ALEX
ROSE	RONALD	ERNESTINE	LYON	HILDA	JESSUP
MICHAEL	LILIAN	LYON		BLACKBURN	
ELIZABETH	LYON				
DAVID					
LYON					

The room also boasts an impressive mahogany dining table which, when extended to its full length, seats 40 guests for dinner. The fine portraits in this room include past and present Earls and family members. In 1931 the Hungarian artist Philip de Laszlo was commissioned on the occasion of their golden wedding anniversary to paint the portraits of the 14th Earl and his Countess Nina Cecilia – parents of The Queen Mother. Other notable portraits include The Queen Mother's grandparents, the 13th Earl and his Countess Frances Dora and her eldest brother, Patrick Lord Glamis, later the 15th Earl.

In 1903 the 13th Earl and Countess celebrated their golden wedding anniversary and, among the many gifts they received, was a magnificent silver galleon which has been the table's centrepiece ever since. Their 11 children presented their parents with the Glamis Lion and their 27 grandchildren gave them a beautiful grandfather clock which still stands in the dining room today. The children's names are engraved on a plaque inside the clock and the names include the three-year-old Elizabeth Bowes Lyon.

Top:
Fergus, 17th Earl
and grandfather of the
present Lord Strathmore.

Above:
Patrick Lord Glamis,
later the 15th Earl.
His striking portrait is by
Glyn Philpot (1884-1937).

Look closely at this beautiful Dutch screen.
Allegedly the spyhole was used by the servants to see when the next course was required at table.

Opposite:
There are many ornate nefs (ship centrepieces) in great houses throughout Scotland. This one was given to the 13th Earl and Countess by the estate tenants to celebrate the couple's golden wedding in 1903. Notice the family coat of arms on the sails.

12

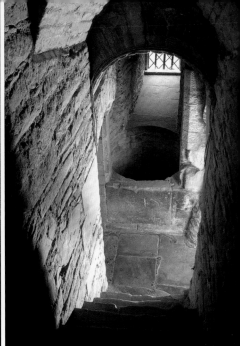

The old well at the
bottom of the stairs was
the Castle's only source
of water, but has long
since dried up. Many
years ago silver plate
and other valuables were
discovered in it.

THE CRYPT

The dramatic front door, dated 1687, leads into the Lower Hall with the
stone spiral staircase giving access to the Crypt. This chamber represents the
ancient heart of the old Castle. Lined with hunting trophies from the Victorian
era, suits of armour and breastplates from darker times, it is also a room that,
legend has it, hides an even darker secret – the Secret Room of Glamis.

It is in the Crypt, in former times, that the family received visitors. Still
echoing around this room are the footsteps of King James VI, King James VIII
and Mary, Queen of Scots.

Renowned furniture maker
The Earl of Snowdon.

This fabulous marquetry
screen of Glamis designed by
him is at the entrance to the
Drawing Room, overleaf.

THE DRAWING ROOM

Above the Crypt was built the Great Hall – now the Drawing Room.

Considered the most splendid apartment in the Castle, it is 60 feet long by 22 feet wide with a fine arched ceiling of beautiful old plasterwork, and bears the monograms of John, 2nd Earl of Kinghorne and his Countess, Margaret Erskine, daughter of the Earl of Mar, and the date, 1621. The room is lit by two great windows cut into the 8 foot thick walls, walls thick enough to hold their own small rooms including the Powder Room, for the powdering of gentlemen's wigs.

The room was not always as elegant – stone walls and a stone barrel-vaulted ceiling lie behind the beautiful stucco plasterwork. It was the 1st Earl who began its transformation and the 2nd Earl continued the process by employing several stuccoists working in the Italian style to embellish the ceiling with plasterwork and to create a frieze. Thus the room evolved from a primitive hall to an elegant Drawing Room.

The great fireplace was built shortly after the 1603 Union of the Crowns. Queen Elizabeth I of England died without issue and King James VI of Scots also became James I, King of England. In the design of the over mantle can be seen the thistles and the roses of the United Kingdom coming together in peace.

Either side of a French ormolu clock are a set of 19th-century porcelain figurines.

The Glamis Lion appears in many forms throughout the Castle. Either side of the fireplace here are two carved giltwood examples once used as candleholders.

SOME PICTURES IN
THE DRAWING ROOM

John Graham of Claverhouse, Viscount Dundee, known as
'Bonnie Dundee' is one of Scotland's most dashing heroes.
A supporter of King James VII and II against King William III,
he raised an army in the Highlands. At a fierce battle in the
Pass of Killiecrankie he defeated General Mackay but, in the
moment of victory, fell mortally wounded. According to
experts, this portrait by Kneller, inspired Sir Walter Scott,
who saw it on his visit here, to describe it in Redgauntlet.
Dundee's seat was at Claverhouse Castle near Glamis;
however, nothing remains of it above ground.

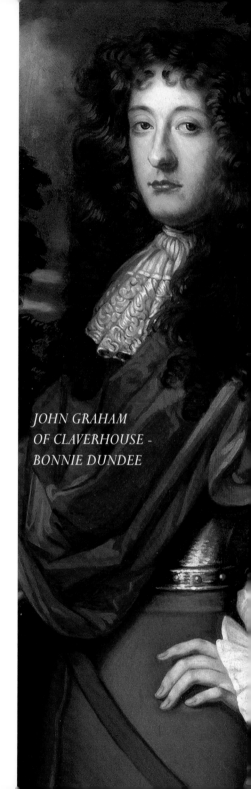

*JOHN GRAHAM
OF CLAVERHOUSE -
BONNIE DUNDEE*

Queen Elizabeth I and King Charles I after Van Dyck

22

THE 3rd EARL

The most striking picture in the room is that of the 3rd Earl with his sons and dogs, and in the distance, his Castle. His father, the 2nd Earl, had been one of the richest peers in Scotland but, at his death, was one of the poorest. As a result, the 3rd Earl inherited property and an estate £40,000 in debt. Over the ensuing 40 years Earl Patrick worked tirelessly to restore both Estate and Castle. Not only did he achieve this, he restored the Strathmore region's pride and prosperity. The picture shows the Castle reconstructed by the Earl, but most of the pictured outer garden walls and gates are now gone.

Painted by Dutch artist Jacob de Wet in 1683, it shows the 3rd Earl surrounded by his sons wearing a fabulous Romanesque tunic, with lion epaulettes. He gestures towards Glamis, the Castle he restored and remodelled to virtually its present 21st century state.

THE CHAPEL

Said to be one of the finest private chapels in northern Europe, it features paintings by the Dutch artist Jacob de Wet, some of which were taken from the Strathmore family Bible.

The most celebrated and extraordinary picture is of Christ wearing a hat. One of only six in the world, it shows Christ and Mary Magdalene in the garden of the sepulchre.

There is a line in St John's Gospel that says when Mary Magdalene saw the resurrected Christ, in the first instance she did not recognise him; she thought he was the gardener. The artist has simply painted Christ as a gardener in a gardener's hat.

DeWet produced several important decorative paintings for the Chapel.

Above: The Last Supper.

Below: The patron saint of Scotland, St Andrew, the fisherman, carrying his catch of two fishes and the traditional x-shaped cross he was crucified on.

A family story relating to the Chapel is that of The Queen Mother's sister, Rose. Rose was to play the organ for the Sunday Service and came in during the week to practice. Opening the door she noticed a lady dressed in grey praying in one of the pews in the otherwise empty Chapel so she waited outside for her to finish. She waited, and waited, but in vain. Finally, looking in, she saw the woman had vanished. What she had witnessed, it is said, was the ghost of Janet Douglas, the Grey Lady of Glamis.

Opposit
An angel gathers Christ's blood and water from the spear wound at h
crucifixion. The image is surrounded by roses and thorns and the thistle
Scotland in this stained glass by Charles Eamer Kemp

THE BILLIARD ROOM

The informal atmosphere of the Billiard
Room is complemented by the five
beautiful tapestries woven by Thomas
Poyntz in the 1680s in the Mortlake style.
The work describes the biblical story of
Nebuchadnezzar of Babylon. Very rare,
the only other known sets are at Powys
in Wales and at Knole in Kent.
There are also fine portraits of Sir
George Bowes and his daughter Mary
Eleanor. His wealth made her one of
the richest heiresses in Europe and in
1767 she married the 9th Earl. The most
striking painting in the room, however, is
the fruit market; a huge Flemish picture
painted in the 1630s by Frans Snyders.
Built in the 18th century, this room was
originally the Library and although many
of the books have been dispersed, some
interesting volumes remain.

Detail from a rare tapestry; one of five in the room.

*A pair of 17th century needleworked panels said
to have been worked by a young girl of the family.*

The idyllic atmosphere of a
market fruit stall is broken
by the intervention of a stray
monkey and a red squirrel
wrestling a basket of peaches
from the table. In this large
picture by Frans Snyders
it is impressive to see how
many varieties of fruit are
on offer; lemons, apples,
pears, artichokes, cherries,
grapes, figs, plums, melons,
pomegranates and many more.

The glory of this room is its plasterwork, especially in the ceiling which bears the monograms of the 2nd Earl of Kinghorne and his first wife Lady Margaret Erskine, together with medallion heads of Roman characters such as Tarquin and Lucretia.

KING MALCOLM'S ROOM

Named in memory of King Malcolm II who died at Glamis in 1034, this room was the private chamber of the Lord and Lady of the house. The exact circumstances surrounding King Malcolm's death remain unknown but different legends suggest his demise resulted from one of the following: assassination, hunting accident or mortal wounds from battle.

In this room hang the embroideries which Lady Helen, wife of the 3rd Earl, and her daughters completed in the year 1683. It is said to have taken them 14 years to make. The room's fine Dutch oak fireplace has an interesting central panel of embossed leather. The dinner service, made for the family in China in the 1770s, was, in 1947, a Royal wedding present to HM The Queen and HRH Prince Philip from the 15th Earl. The Queen and Prince Philip graciously returned the china to Glamis to ensure this great collection stayed complete.

THE ROYAL CONNECTION

*An intimate study of The Queen Mother's
writing bureau, situated in the corner of
'The Queen Mother's Sitting Room', the
main room in The Royal Suite, or Apartments.
The room is very much as it was left by The
Queen Mother, with treasured photographs
of her family.*

THE ROYAL APARTMENTS

French night-light clock.

One of the decorative English tiles in the fireplace.

In 1923 the Countess converted this part of the Castle into private apartments for her daughter and son-in-law, Their Royal Highnesses The Duke and Duchess of York (later King George VI and Queen Elizabeth). Until their Coronation in 1937 the rooms were used by them on their many visits to Glamis and remain relatively unchanged. The sitting room contains many family photographs including a signed photograph of Princess Margaret who was born here at Glamis in 1930. There is a magnificent German oak press (armoire) which has fascinating detail carved into its columns and four corners. In the corner of the room stands a beautiful Italian cabinet, delightfully decorated with glass ceramics and lapis lazuli.

In the Royal bedroom, the most interesting item is the great four-poster bed which was embroidered lovingly over many years by The Queen Mother's mother, Countess Cecilia. The names of her ten children can be seen inside the canopy. 'Michael 1893' refers to the great grandfather of the present Earl and 'Elizabeth 1900' to Her Majesty Queen Elizabeth The Queen Mother.

HM Queen Elizabeth The Queen Mother portrayed in her favourite and immediately recognisable colour scheme of powder blue. Oil on canvas by Michael Noakes.

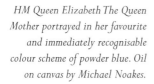

Embroidered and presented by the Countess of Strathmore to her husband, the 14th Earl, on the occasion of their golden wedding in 1931.

THE KING'S ROOM

The final room in the Royal
Apartments is the King's Room.
It looks like a bedroom but was
in fact King George VI's study and
dressing room and contains one
of the oldest and most valuable
pieces of furniture in the Castle,
the Kinghorne bed, made c.1660
for the 3rd Earl.

Another fine piece of furniture
here is the 'Semainier'. The name
comes from the French 'semaine',
meaning week. The drawers
represented the days of the week
for your clothes, thus your best
clothes for Sunday were always in
the 'top drawer'.

*The bed has had many famous
occupants, particularly The Old
Pretender, Bonnie Prince Charlie's
father. It is said that he left in such
a great hurry in the morning to catch
a boat to France, that he forgot his
watch. The maid came to turn down
the bed, found the watch and took it
home. Her family had it for almost
100 years but eventually they returned
it to the Castle and it is now on
display in the Exhibition Room.*

THE QUEEN MOTHER
AND GLAMIS

'Duty is the rent you pay for life'

Opposite: HM Queen Elizabeth The Queen Mother with the 18th Earl of Strathmore and Kinghorne in the grounds of Clarence House, after a State Opening of Parliament. Lord Strathmore is wearing the uniform of a Captain of the Yeoman of the Guard.

The Queen Mother was born Elizabeth Bowes Lyon in the final year of Queen Victoria's reign and in her lifetime she witnessed the reigns of six monarchs and the term of office of 20 Prime Ministers.

The Queen Mother's father, Claude, 14th Earl, portrayed by de László in the robes of a Knight of The Garter.

Elizabeth's parents were Lord and Lady Glamis. Her father, Claude, was heir to the ancient Scottish Earldom of Strathmore and Kinghorne. Her mother, Nina Cecilia Cavendish Bentinck, was of the family of the Dukes of Portland. Her family home was, in 1900, St Paul's Walden Bury in Hertfordshire. Glamis Castle was, at the time, the home of Elizabeth's grandfather, the 13th Earl.

Some mystery still surrounds exactly where Elizabeth was born, but we know she was not born at Glamis as is sometimes mistakenly assumed. It was long thought she was born at St Paul's Walden Bury, but it is now believed that she was born in London, perhaps at the family's town house. Elizabeth was the ninth of ten children. The first-born, Violet Hyacinth, whom The Queen Mother never knew, had died tragically in 1893 of a heart problem caused by diphtheria. She was aged 11. When Elizabeth arrived on 4 August 1900, the ages of the other children, Mary, Patrick, Jock, Alexander, Fergus, Rose and Michael ranged from 17 down to seven years. Her brother Patrick, as eldest son, would later become the 15th Earl of Strathmore and Kinghorne.

Lady Glamis was a doting mother to all her children and rather than employ a wet nurse, as was the norm, she breast-fed Elizabeth for 18 months. She was the keystone of the family, much loved by all her children and staff but she was still very Victorian in the values she instilled into her children. 'Duty is the rent you pay for life', was one of her favourite maxims. It was one that Elizabeth would hear often as she grew up. When Elizabeth was two, her mother surprised everyone by producing David, her tenth and last child. Elizabeth and David were nicknamed 'my two Benjamins' – Benjamin being the name of the youngest son of Jacob in the Bible. David soon became Elizabeth's inseparable childhood companion and they did everything together as if they were twins. When Elizabeth was four her grandfather, the 13th Earl, died and her father inherited the Earldom, and with it, Glamis Castle. Elizabeth was now 'Lady Elizabeth' and the family thereafter divided their time between Glamis, St Paul's Walden Bury and Streatlam Castle in County Durham.

Elizabeth and David were full of pranks and mischief. Pouring 'boiling oil', which was actually icy water, from the ramparts on arriving guests was one such prank. Another was the placing of a football under the wheels of the family motor car so that it would explode and frighten the chauffeur. Lady Elizabeth celebrated her 14th birthday on 4 August 1914 and en route to the birthday treat – a vaudeville show in London – the streets suddenly filled with people. The crowds were cheering and waving flags. Then, at the end of the show, the theatre manager came onto the stage to announce that war had been declared on Germany that very evening. Soon after, Lady Elizabeth, her mother and her sister Rose, returned to Glamis where the Castle was converted to a convalescent home for wounded soldiers.

The Queen Mother's eldest brother of six, Patrick, Lord Glamis, served as an Officer in the Scots Guards during the Great War. He later became 15th Earl.

This richly decorated banner is one of many which hung on London's Mall at the Coronation of The Queen Mother, and signifies and celebrates the union of two families; the Royal family on the left-hand side, with the three lions of England, the Welsh harp and the Scottish lion, and the Bowes Lyon arms on the right. Today it graces the Glamis Castle restaurant.

When the first casualties arrived, Elizabeth found herself immersed in their care and welfare. This was to be her role throughout the war but it was one at which she excelled. Her kindness won her the hearts of many of the soldiers who passed through Glamis. On 16 September 1916 two soldiers discovered a fire in a room under the Castle roof. As they ran to raise the alarm, the first person they came across was Lady Elizabeth who showed great presence of mind and immediately telephoned both the local and Dundee fire brigades. She then marshalled everyone to fight the fire, organising a chain to convey buckets of water from the river. Later, with the fire raging above them, she organised the removal of the valuables out onto the lawn. In 1918 the armistice signalled the end of the war and the end of an era. Once the last soldier had left Glamis in 1919, Lady Elizabeth was launched into the high society of the day at her 'coming out' party.

Lady Elizabeth and Prince Albert, the second son of King George V and Queen Mary, first met at a children's party in London when she was five and he was ten. Fifteen years later, whilst at a ball in London, Elizabeth caught the eye of the Prince once again when he saw her dancing with his equerry, James Stuart. Prince Albert later confided to Lady Airlie that he had fallen in love that very evening, but he did not realise it until some time later. 'Bertie' proposed to Elizabeth in the spring of 1921 when she was 20 and he was 25. When she refused him, he was disconsolate although they did continue to see each other. A further proposal followed, and then on 5 January 1923 the Daily News headlined 'Scottish bride for the Prince of Wales' – but the tabloid had got it wrong. It was not the Prince of Wales but the Duke of York who was wooing Elizabeth.

A few days later, Bertie proposed again and this time was accepted. The telegraph he sent to his parents said simply 'Alright – Bertie.' The Court Circular of 13 January 1923 announced: 'It is with the greatest pleasure that the King and Queen announce the betrothal of their beloved son the Duke of York to the Lady Elizabeth Bowes Lyon'. Sir Henry Channon wrote in his diary: 'There is not a man in England who does not envy him'.

The Royal wedding took place in Westminster Abbey on 26 April 1923, the first to be held there since 1382. The Royal couple spent some of their honeymoon at Glamis. She soon settled into her new life and gave her husband the confidence and support he needed in the events which were soon to engulf them and bring him unexpectedly to the throne and she to the position of Queen Consort. On 21 April 1926, she gave birth, in London, to their first child, Princess Elizabeth, our present Queen. Then, on a stormy August night at Glamis in 1930, Princess Margaret was born – the first Royal baby to be born in Scotland since the year 1602.

In 1936 King George V died and Bertie's older brother David became King Edward VIII. Later that same year the King abdicated in favour of his brother Bertie who accepted the burden of duty as King George VI. Then, and through the long, dark days of the Second World War the Queen, affectionately known as 'the little Scots lass from Glamis' was to prove her worth. She more than fulfilled her mother's maxim that 'duty is the rent you pay for life.'

Commemorative panel, displayed at Glamis, celebrating the Coronation of King George VI, with his Duchess as Queen Consort.

HRH THE PRINCESS MARGARET AND GLAMIS

On 21 August 1930, Princess Margaret Rose was born at Glamis Castle. At the news of the birth, and despite a raging storm, local people built a huge bonfire on the hill above the village to celebrate. In accordance with a 300-year-old custom, the Home Secretary had to attend the birth to verify the identity of this Royal child. Her sister Lilibet (the present Queen) nicknamed her 'Bud', as she was not a fully-grown Rose!

The family led a very happy life, dividing their time between London, the Bowes Lyon ancestral homes and other Royal residences. The long summer holidays spent in Glamis were very special to Princess Margaret and she frequently returned to the place of her birth through the years.

In 1952 her father, King George VI, died and a year later she attended the Coronation of her sister, Elizabeth, at Westminster Abbey, where she was crowned Queen Elizabeth II. In 1960 Margaret married society photographer Antony Armstrong-Jones. They had two children, Viscount Linley, who has now succeeded his father as earl of Snowdon, and Lady Sarah Armstrong-Jones.

The memorial to HRH The Princess Margaret, completed in 2006, was designed by the 18th Earl and Fred Stephens, architect. It is made from stone quarried in County Durham and was constructed by Watson and Sons stonemasons of St Andrews.

Opposite: A proud and happy mother with her two daughters: HM The Queen, HM Queen Elizabeth The Queen Mother and HRH The Princess Margaret in the celebrated photograph 'The Blue Trinity, 1980' by favourite family photographer, Norman Parkinson. ©Norman Parkinson Archive

Princess Margaret died in February 2002 at the age of 71. Prayers were said in the family chapel here at Glamis. During the funeral service in St George's Chapel Windsor, many of her achievements were remembered: her active support of the Guide Movement, the Arts, the Royal Ballet and the NSPCC. Her funeral was held on the 50th anniversary of her father's funeral and occurred during the Queen's Golden Jubilee year. The ceremony was a family occasion and it also marked the last time The Queen Mother was seen in public before her own death, some weeks later. A full state memorial service followed but, unlike other members of the Royal family Princess Margaret was cremated, allowing her ashes to be placed in the tomb of her beloved parents at Windsor Castle.

This Royal Princess will be remembered as a character of great vivacity and a woman of great beauty.

GHOSTLY GLAMIS

It is said that Glamis Castle is the most haunted castle in Scotland, if not the United Kingdom. There are many myths and legends attached to Glamis but the ones which are most vividly described concern a pageboy, two Lords and a Lady.

The ghost of a little pageboy sits on the stone seat just inside The Queen Mother's Sitting Room. He was renowned for his mischief and was often told to sit there for punishment. On the coldest night of the coldest winter everyone retired to their beds, forgetting to dismiss the little boy from his seat. For once he obeyed an order and remained seated upon the stone. Sadly, during the night he froze to death and was found the next morning still in his seat. Today, his ghost, still vengeful, has a habit of putting out a foot to trip up the unwary as they enter the room – a sure sign his mischievousness has returned!

The secret chamber at Glamis has given rise to many a legend and theory. The favourite tale is that of an early Lord Glamis and his old enemy the Earl of Crawford – known as 'Tiger' due to his temper. They gambled through Saturday evening late into the night and were disturbed by the servants at midnight who begged them to stop playing as the Sabbath was now upon them. 'We care not what day of the week it is,' roared the Lords. 'If we have

a mind to we shall play until Doomsday.' As the first cards hit the table early that Sunday morning the door creaked open and there stood the Devil. 'I will take your Lordships at your word', he said. 'Doomsday has come for both of you.' They still play and it is said that if you listen at the walls of the room at midnight on Saturdays you can often hear the two Lords sobbing, and the shuffling of cards.

No visitor to Glamis can feel anything but sympathy for the Grey Lady who is said to haunt the Chapel. She was, in life, Janet Douglas wife of the 6th Lord Glamis and when he died only a few years after their marriage she found herself victimised by King James V. He wanted the Castle and he hated the Douglas family – she stood no chance. He falsely accused her of witchcraft, her two small sons of treason and all three were imprisoned in Edinburgh Castle. There were riots in Edinburgh, such was the outrage of the people. They knew the accusations were false. Eventually, the King had Janet tried for, convicted of, and executed for witchcraft. She was burnt alive at the stake on Castle Hill in front of Edinburgh Castle in 1537 and her spirit upon her death returned to Glamis. 151 years later she was seen entering the then new Chapel where she has her own seat and where she quietly prays for eternal peace. She is the most frequently seen ghost at Glamis.

Duncan's Hall built in the brutal 1400s was for centuries the guard room of the Castle where people would arrive, present their credentials, surrender their weapons and then, move on, unarmed, into the castle.

The medieval 'Big Brother' spyhole (right), is evidence of that nervousness. There is also this bear. He came to Glamis as a family pet from North America in the 1820s.

GRUESOME GLAMIS – THE STORY OF MACBETH

In 1040 Macbeth was crowned King at Scone, near Perth. His reign of
17 years is often viewed negatively: 'I think our country sinks beneath
the yoke, it weeps, it bleeds and each new day a gash is added to her
wounds'. (William Shakespeare's 'Macbeth'). Centuries after his life
had passed into legend and folklore, many historians, such as Ralph
Holinshed, began to blacken his name. Shakespeare was influenced
by Holinshed's 'Chronicles', and by the stories he heard at King James'
court in London. Wanting to please the new King, and, perhaps
influenced by past events at Glamis (the death of King Malcolm - who
was the grandfather of Duncan and Macbeth), Shakespeare wrote
'The Scottish Play'. Ever the politician, Shakespeare included some
of the family names of the King's favourites, setting the gruesome
murder at the Castle of the Thane of Glamis, ie Macbeth. Since
Shakespeare's time, the old guardroom here at Glamis has been
known as Duncan's Hall in commemoration of that tragedy.

Legends have described Macbeth as 'luxurious, avaricious, false,
deceitful, sudden, malicious and smacking of every sin that has a
name'. In truth he was a rightful claimant to the Scottish throne
and seems to have spent a considerable amount of his time quelling
regional and clan rebellions in the north and repulsing invading bands
of Vikings.

The carriage at Glamis is described as a 'Brightons Chair' on the invoice (right). This was an invalid carriage; effectively a horse-drawn wheelchair, and was purchased for the 13th Earl's mother to use in later life. Similarly, more urban vehicles of the era, were called phaetons. The name 'phaeton' derives from the classical tale of mythical Phaeton, son of Helios, who set the earth on fire while attempting to drive the chariot of the sun.

THIS 'BRIGHTONS CHAIR' IS TO BE SEEN AT THE END OF THE CASTLE TOUR IN THE CRYPT ALCOVE

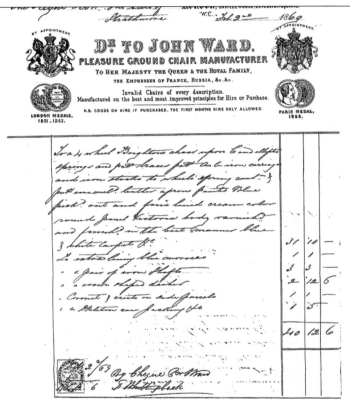

This is a copy of the original invoice for this BRIGHTONS CHAIR purchased by the 13th Earl of Strathmore in 1869. It cost £40:12s:6d.

To a 4 wheel Brightons chair upon Candelliptie springs and patent braces patent axle iron carriage and iron stocks to wheels spring cushion patent enamel'd leather aprons painted blue pick'd out and fine lined cream color round panel Victoria body varnish'd and finish'd in the best manner blue & white carpet &c.   31:10:-

To extra lining blue morocco	1: 1:-
" a pair of iron shafts	3: 3:-
" a crown shaped dasher	2:12:6
" coronet & crests on side panels	1: 1:-
" a skeleton case packing etc	1: 5:-
	40:12:6

Two of the stunningly convincing and intricate rooms of Glamis Castle in the Doll's House

GLAMIS GALLERY

The exhibition room within the Castle contains a colourful array of photographs, costumes and memorabilia of the family, regional history and heritage. Perhaps the most intriguing item in the collection is the King's watch (see The King's Room in The Royal Apartments). Beside the watch is the sword which The Old Pretender gave as a token of appreciation for his short stay. However, in view of the fact that James was accompanied by 88 followers, it was not exactly the biggest reward for the hospitality the family had extended.

Patrick, 3rd Earl (1643–1695) was the last nobleman in Scotland to retain the services of a private buffoon or jester. The jester's motley (costume) is preserved in the Castle and can be seen in the Drawing Room, and a small copy worn by The Queen Mother's brother when a boy, can be seen here.

Bullet-proof leather jerkin which once belonged to the charismatic and dashing John Graham of Claverhouse, known as 'Bonnie Dundee' (see the Drawing Room).

18th century plaid uniform of the Royal Company of Archers (The Queen's Bodyguard in Scotland).

This Victorian calamander vanity case was made in 1882–83 and is fitted with 11 cut-glass jars and bottles with silver gilt mounts engraved with the monogram CFB; Constance Frances Blackburn. The case was a wedding gift to his eldest daughter, Constance, from the 13th Earl. This delightful piece can be seen in the Glamis Exhibition area.

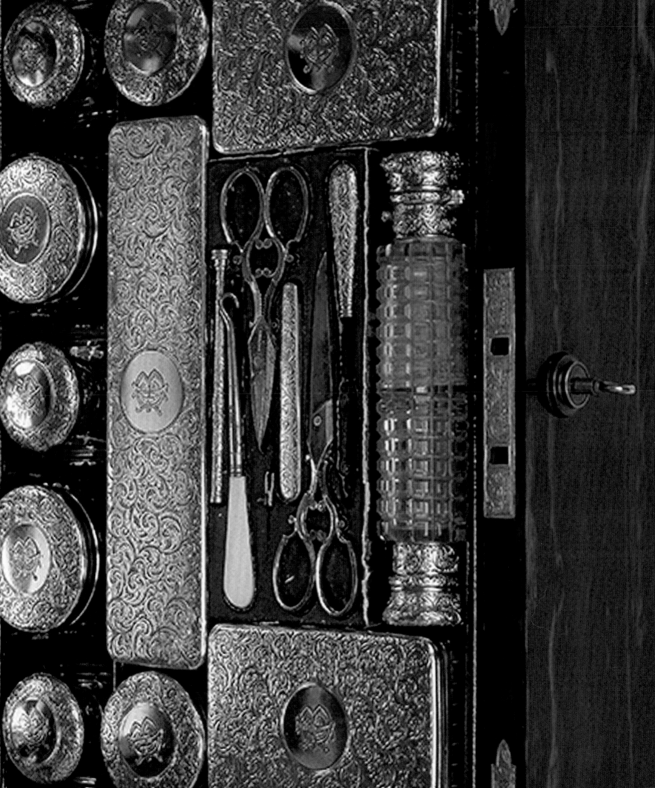

THE GARDENS

There is evidence of planting and landscaping at Glamis stretching back some five centuries. At the time the Castle was surrounded by extensive walled gardens, which were created by the 3rd Earl in the late 17th century and seen in Jacob de Wet's portrait of him which hangs in the Drawing Room. These were swept away by the 9th Earl at the end of the 18th century and replaced by an extensive landscape park. Much of the planting which provides the setting for the Castle today, including many fine conifers, was instigated by the 13th Earl after 1865.

Today the main areas of interest are:

Each of these areas has its own character and specific flora and fauna and visitors to Glamis are encouraged to enjoy each and every one.

THE FORECOURT AND DUTCH GARDEN

Maps of the 18th century and pictures of the same period show this area as an enclosed courtyard flanked by two rectangular walled gardens. The corners of these gardens were marked by the two circular turrets which still stand on the lawns in front of the Castle. Surviving parts of the old gardens include the 17th century sundial, the two statues at the foot of the Avenue, and two old yew trees which stood in what was once known as the 'flower garden'.

The garden walls were taken down in the 1770s. The small sunken garden on one side of the forecourt, known as the Dutch Garden, was created in 1893 to designs by Arthur Castings of London. It is laid out in a formal way with flower beds bounded by low box hedges, and with a small statue of Mercury, Messenger of the Gods, as its focal point. The garden is private but can be easily viewed from the Castle forecourt.

Opposite: An artist's impression of the Dutch Garden, laid out by the 13th Earl (left) in 1893, and right, how remarkably unchanged it is today.

Piper Jimmy Doig

THE AVENUE

The mile-long avenue to the Castle is lined with great oaks first planted by Patrick, 3rd Earl, in the 17th century. Before the approach stand The Queen Mother Memorial Gates, opened in 2008 by HRH The Prince Charles The Duke of Rothesay, accompanied by HRH The Duchess of Rothesay. The gates, funded by public subscription, together with the new approach allow, for the first time in history, a view of the Castle from Glamis village.

At one time the approach to the Castle was made through a series of grand ornamental gateways set at intervals along the avenue – as seen in the 3rd Earl's portrait hanging in the Drawing Room (see illustration right). These gateways were removed in 1775 and rebuilt around the edge of the policies.

A second great avenue crossed the main approach to the Castle at right angles (see right). Several old lime trees in the car park, and a few old trees at the foot of the sunken wall or ha-ha which separates the gardens from the policies, are all that remain of the 3rd Earl's planting.

THE ITALIAN GARDEN

The Italian Garden to the east of the
Castle was laid out by Countess Cecilia,
c.1910 to designs by Arthur Castings.
Bounded by yew hedges, this garden
includes a raised terrace between
two small gazebos, from which can be
seen fan-shaped parterres of formal
beds separated by gravel walks. Other
features include pleached alleys of
beech, a stone fountain and ornamental
gates which commemorate The Queen
Mother's 80th birthday.

THE ITALIAN GARDEN

The Walled Garden is a hidden gem. Once used to produce fruit and vegetables for the Castle, it had fallen into disuse in recent times. However with the close personal involvement of The 18th Earl and Countess a major redevelopment began in 2008 with new plantings and the installation of a spectacular fountain. As the late Earl's work continues to mature a visit to the Walled garden has become an integral part of any visit to Glamis Castle.

In the burn are salmon and other game fish. There are dippers and kingfishers around the water's edge and, on the wider estate, there is often an osprey nest and other birds associated with this part of Scotland. Butterflies and bees grace the gardens in summer and there are usually several types present, some of which are rare. Wild areas and patches of nettles are deliberately left to encourage butterflies and other wildlife such as roe deer and hares.

Clockwise from top left: Otter, Dipper, Kingfisher, Bee, Scotch Argus Butterfly, Black Grouse, Osprey.
All photographs by Mark Hamblin, Carrbridge.

GLAMIS GEOGRAPHY
THE VILLAGE & ESTATE

Evidence of man's habitation around Glamis can be traced back to the Picts. From the 4th–9th century AD, they controlled virtually all of Scotland. The carved standing stone in the manse garden, from around the 9th century, is an excellent example of their work. Later, Glamis became a centre for the conversion of the Picts to Christianity. St Fergus, Patron Saint of Glamis, travelled across from Ireland in the early 8th century, establishing the church as he went, before choosing Glamis as his place of rest. He is said to have lived in a cave on the banks of the Glamis Burn and made use of a nearby spring to baptise the early converts to Christianity.

It was not until the early 14th century that Glamis once again began to play a significant role in Scottish history. After the capture and destruction of Forfar Castle from English forces by Robert the Bruce, the King and Court had to reside a few miles away at the Royal hunting lodge in Glamis.

In 1242, David, Bishop of St Andrew's, dedicated a church to St Fergus on the site of the present kirk. In the 15th century Lady Glamis built the Strathmore Aisle onto this building, with the family burial vault beneath, which was used until 1865. The Strathmore Aisle remains to this day although the original kirk was demolished in 1790 to make way for the present one. The graveyard also tells a story. The earliest tombstone is dated 1630. Others tell the story of masons, weavers, farmers, brewers, bakers, metal workers and many other trades, through pictorial representation. The grave of Margaret Bridie is also to be seen. She made bridies (meat pasties) famous. However, Glamis has had little credit for her efforts as they became popular as 'Forfar Bridies'.

'Whenever throughout Scotland there rose towers of a castle there was found the humble houses of a hamlet or village built under the shadow of the great pile'. To this rule Glamis was no exception. The retainers and dependants of the Lords of Glamis, those who owed feudal service and allegiance, formed the early village community. In 1491, James IV made Glamis a 'burgh of barony' and allowed it the privilege of holding a public 'fayre' annually on the feast day of St Fergus (17 November). Hence Glamis became a country town of considerable importance.

A plan dated 1773 shows the village much as it exists today except for the Kirkwynd Cottages built in 1793, and the recent development to the west of the Dundee–Kirriemuir road. Many of the current houses date from the late 18th century and early 19th century. The Manse dates from 1788, and the School from 1839. In the late 18th–19th century the main industry was the flax trade. A spinning mill was built in 1806, employing 66. In 1836 the population of the village was 2,050; in 1910 it was 1,159 and in 1993 it had reduced to 790.

The village of Glamis has great charm and is well worth a visit. Amongst many features of interest are the church and the Pictish carved stone. Close by is the ancient St Fergus Well and an attractive walk along the river.

The Gin Bothy

St Fergus Church and the Pictish standing stone c. 9th–10th century.

St Fergus Well

Head Forester at work

Water Wheel

The Head Gamekeeper

Both the Castle and the village are the focus of a traditional country estate which today supports and encourages the development of a thriving rural community.

The Estate has developed over many centuries and today comprises a wide variety of properties and business and leisure activities. The policy has always been to maintain and restore the traditional parts of the Estate, whilst at the same time supporting and encouraging the community.

Strathmore's diverse farming business is looked after by the Farms Director and extends to approx 2000 ha. This diverse business includes quality pork and beef production with arable crops of cereals, vegetables and root crops all managed alongside a variety of rural stewardship and conservation measures designed to help the environment. Once again, although the most modern tractors and machinery are used to produce the food, great care is taken to enhance and conserve the wildlife habitats in hedgerows and field margins which are so important in today's modern agriculture.

Much of the village of Glamis was built by the Earl of Strathmore around 1760 and the policy, as with all dwellings, is to maintain the character of these buildings whilst providing modern accommodation for those living in the rural community. The woods on the Estate have remained in continuous forestry for many centuries and, on a plan dated 1788, have almost identical boundaries to the present day. There is thus a wide range of tree species with some large and very spectacular ancient trees. On a rural estate all the various activities influence and affect each other and the best example of this is the wildlife and sporting shooting. The pheasant shooting employs several gamekeepers and part-time staff and attracts visiting guests from the UK and overseas. The income from this allows funds to be available which benefit all other forms of wildlife by enabling the Estate to retain rough areas which

are not planted with commercial trees and areas of crop planted especially for some birds rather than being sown with a crop of barley. When areas of forestry are being replanted, open areas can be left and a proportion of hardwood trees planted to diversify the forest for the benefit of wildlife. Like other estates, the Strathmore Estate encourages a diversity of businesses in order to provide employment in the countryside.

The Estate is fortunate to have a large tourism operation centred on the Castle which brings in many tens of thousands of visitors each year and, in so doing, supports many jobs throughout the county of Angus in local hotels, bed and breakfasts, restaurants and other businesses. Along with the formal gardens and grounds of the Castle, public access is encouraged on the other parts of the Estate. Both locals and visitors alike can relax, exercise dogs and enjoy the wildlife which surrounds them. The Estate will continue to benefit and encourage a great number of people, both employed here and those completely outside the Estate, who wish to live and work in the country.

GLAMIS GENEALOGY
FAMILY HISTORY

'I must own,' wrote Sir Walter Scott when he stayed a night at Glamis, 'that when I heard door after door shut, after my conductor had retired, I began to consider myself as too far from the living, and somewhat too near the dead'. Scott's feelings were understandable – Glamis reeks of history and is peopled with phantoms, be they genuine echoes of past occurrences, or the figments of imaginations held in thrall by the very stones which have witnessed nearly 700 years of Scotland's history.

As far back as the 8th century Glamis was a holy place. St Fergus came from Ireland to preach and is said to have lived and died here. A number of Celtic stones in the vicinity date from this period and St Fergus' Well is close to the kirk. Many members of the Strathmore family have borne the name of the saint.

Bowes

Lyon

Sir John Lyon of Glamis (d.1382) = Princess Joanna dau. of King Robert II

Sir John Lyon of Glamis (d.1435)

Patrick, 1st Lord Glamis (d.1459)

Alexander, 2nd Lord Glamis (d.1486)　　John, 3rd Lord Glamis (d.1497)

John, 4th Lord Glamis (d.1500)

George, 5th Lord Glamis (d. unm. 1505)　　John, 6th Lord Glamis (d.1528)

John, 7th Lord Glamis (d.1559)

John, 8th Lord Glamis (d.1578)

Patrick, 1st Earl of Kinghorne (1575–1615)

John, 2nd Earl of Kinghorne (1596–1646)

Patrick, 3rd Earl of Strathmore and Kinghorne (1643–1695)

John, 4th Earl of Strathmore (1663–1712)

John, 5th Earl (dsp 1715)　　Charles, 6th Earl (dsp 1728)　　James, 7th Earl (dsp 1735)　　Thomas, 8th Earl of Strathmore (1704–1753)

John, 9th Earl of Strathmore (1737–1776)= Mary Bowes

John, 10th Earl (dsp 1820)　　Thomas, 11th Earl of Strathmore (1773–1846)

John Bowes (1811 - 1885)　　Thomas, Lord Glamis

Thomas, 12th Earl (dsp 1865)　　Claude, 13th Earl of Strathmore (1824–1904)

Claude, 14th Earl of Strathmore, K.G., K.T., G.C.V.O. (1855–1944)
= Nina Cecilia Cavendish Bentinck

Patrick, 15th Earl of Strathmore (1884–1949)　　Hon. Michael Bowes Lyon　　4 brothers and 3 sisters　　Lady Elizabeth Bowes Lyon = HM King George VI

John, Master of Glamis (k. in action 1941)　　Timothy Patrick 16th Earl (1918–1972) m Mary Brennan (1923 - 1967)　　Fergus, 17th Earl of Strathmore and Kinghorne (1928–1987) = Mary Pamela McCorquodale, Dowager Countess of Strathmore and Kinghorne (b. 1932)　　HM Queen Elizabeth II　　HRH The Princess Margaret

Lady Caroline Frances (1959 - 1960)

Michael Fergus, 18th Earl of Strathmore and Kinghorne (1957–2016) = (m iii 2012) Karen Rose, Countess of Strathmore and Kinghorne　　Lady Elizabeth Bowes Lyon (b. 1959) = Antony Leeming　　Lady Diana Bowes Lyon (b. 1966) = Christopher Godfrey-Faussett

= (m i 1984) Isobel Countess of Strathmore and Kinghorne (m diss 2004)　　= (m ii 2005) Damaris Stuart-William (m diss 2008)

Simon Patrick 19th Earl of Strathmore and Kinghorne (b. 1986)　　Hon. John Fergus Bowes Lyon (b. 1988)　　Hon. George Norman Bowes Lyon (b. 1991)　　Hon. Toby Peter Fergus Bowes Lyon (b. 2005)

From earliest known records Glamis belonged to the Scottish crown. It was not originally a fortress, which is why it stands on low-lying ground in the midst of the lush Angus landscape. Its original purpose was a hunting lodge for the Kings of Scots who doubtless enjoyed many a good day out in the thick forests which must, at that time, have existed here. Its position on boggy ground, however, would have provided some defence.

The Royal Hunting Lodge
as it may have appeared pre-1404

When the three witches approached Macbeth, hailing him as 'Thane of Cawdor and of Glamis', Shakespeare was guilty of a solecism as neither Glamis nor Cawdor are known to have been Thanages in the 11th century. Glamis makes its first appearance as a Thanage in 1264, a thane being a Lord holding his lands of the Crown subject to the Scots customs of landholding at that time. Thanages were gradually phased out to be substituted by Norman-style baronies after the death of Alexander III. Thus Robert II changed Glamis from a Thanage to a feudal barony (not to be confused with the English peerage title) in 1376, when he granted it to Sir John Lyon. King Malcolm II died here at Glamis in 1034. He was succeeded by Duncan I, the son of his elder daughter, who was slain near Elgin (probably in battle) by his first cousin Macbeth (the son of Malcolm's younger daughter), in 1040. Macbeth, in turn, met a sticky end and, although Shakespeare makes a great drama out of it, these events were not uncommon in the turbulent Scotland of those days when Kings of Scots were frequently slain by their heirs.

The story moves on to the year 1372 when Robert II, the first Stewart King of Scots, granted to Sir John Lyon of Forteviot the Thanage of Glamis for services to the Crown. Four years later Sir John married the King's daughter, Princess Joanna Stewart. Sir John was later appointed Chamberlain of Scotland – at that time the most important office at the disposal of the Crown. The King, having raised the thanage of Glamis into a feudal barony, granted it to his son-in-law – the reddendo (payment) was a red falcon to be presented annually to the King at Pentecost.

The origin of the Lyon family name is uncertain – some say from the Norman invasion, some say from the Clan Lamont. However, this Sir John was known as 'The White Lion' perhaps because of his very fair hair and pale skin. Therefore his coat of arms was a blue lion rampant (possibly as a pun on his name and as a special mark of Royal favour). This was later enclosed in what is known in heraldry as a 'double tressure flory counter flory' – a decorative surround similar to that borne on the present royal arms of Scotland and known in Scotland as an augmentation – 'a royal tressure'.

The first Sir John was knighted in 1377 and founded the line of feudal Barons and later Earls which continues to this day. Sir John met a violent end at the hands of Sir James Lindsay of Crawford, Scotland's ambassador to England. It is said that he was undiplomatically murdered in his bed. His son, the second Sir John Lyon, began building the Castle as we know it today, c.1400. It is thought that he built the east wing – now housing the Royal Apartments – after his marriage to the great-granddaughter of King Robert II. Access to the Castle at this time was probably by an external stair to the first floor.

His son, Patrick Lyon, was created a peer of Parliament in 1445 as Lord Glamis after being released by the English who had held him hostage for King James I of Scots. He became a Privy Councillor and Master of the Household in 1450. It is said he began to build the Great Tower c.1435 which was completed by his widow in 1484. It was not linked to the east wing for another one hundred years.

The Palace House c.1404 built by Sir John Lyon

The Great Tower, built in the shape of an 'L', was a tall building, typical of many similar castles then being built throughout Scotland – primitive by later standards but fairly impregnable to attack.

There would have been a cellar on the ground floor and an entrance hall on the next which was reached by outer stairs. The second floor contained the Great Hall where the lord and his family would live and dine. Surrounding the Castle was a fortified court.

Tragedy struck the family after the death of John, 6th Lord Glamis, who had married a Douglas: tragedy, because of what happened to his widow.

King James V, as a child, had been dominated by his Douglas stepfather and had been manipulated by other members of the clan. As King he became obsessive in his hatred of the Douglas family and carried on a ruthless vendetta against them. Poor Lady Campbell (Lady Glamis had remarried), a woman of impeccable character, of singular beauty and popularity, did not escape the King's ferocity. A trumped-up charge of witchcraft was brought against her and she was condemned to be burnt at the stake as a witch. After long imprisonment in a dark dungeon within Edinburgh Castle, she was almost blind. In 1537 she was taken out to the Castle gates, tied to a stake, and burnt alive. Even her young son, the 7th Lord Glamis, was condemned to death and imprisoned, only to be released after the King had died.

Not content with this grave atrocity, the King considered Glamis Castle as forfeit to the Crown, occupied it and held Court there from 1537 to 1542. Many existing Royal decrees and charters are dated from the Castle during this period. These events suggest the Castle was a comfortable and desirable place at the time.

When the young 7th Lord Glamis was released after James V's death and restored to his property by Act of Parliament, he found that the Royal usurpers had plundered his home of all its most valuable things – silver, bedding and furniture

had all been taken away. A happier event took place years after when, in 1562, the daughter of the cruel James V visited Glamis and showed great favour to the family, perhaps as reparation for her father's wickedness. She was, of course, Mary, Queen of Scots.

The Queen was on her way north to be present in person at the quelling of a rebellion led by the Earl of Huntly. She was accompanied by her four Marys, her ladies-in-waiting, who made a new tapestry chair cover to while away the time. The English ambassador who was present wrote to Queen Elizabeth I that in spite of 'extreme Fowle and Colde weather, I never saw her merrier, never dismayed'.

The 8th Lord Glamis was Chancellor of Scotland and Keeper of the Great Seal. By the end of the 16th century he was described by the English ambassador as having 'the greatest revenue of any baron in Scotland, and of being 'very wise and discreet'. At about this time the household consisted of 'a principal servitor and maister stabular, two servitors, a musicianer, maister cook and browster (for the bakehouse and brewhouse respectively), foremen, a maister porter and his servant, a grieve and an officer'. The lady of the house would be attended by '2 gentlewomen, a browdinstar (embroiderer), a lotrix (bedmaker) and two other female servants'. Like his forebear, Sir John Lyon, Lord Glamis, met his death at the hands of followers of the Lindsay family, though this time it was by accident.

His son, 9th Lord Glamis, bore the Christian name of Patrick which was to become so popular with his successors. He, too, became a Privy Councillor having succeeded to the title and property as an infant of three. When only eight years old and while travelling in France, the young master of Glamis had his portrait painted by a follower of the painter François Clouet. On the reverse is a portrait of the 16-year-old George Boswell, his secretary.

The 9th Lord Glamis was created Earl of Kinghorne by James VI in 1606. His title probably relates to the grant by Robert II to Sir John Lyon in 1381, of the burgh of Kinghorne, in Fife, with the manor place, lands, rents and forests belonging to the King. This higher rank of peerage in some way redressed the wrong done to the Lyon family by James V. Kinghorne became one of the King's Privy Councillors and accompanied his sovereign south when he succeeded as James I of England. It is at the English Court that he might have met Shakespeare. The newly appointed Earl continued the long process of evolving the architecture of the Castle to a semblance of what it is today by remodelling the tower and stair turret between 1600 and 1606.

The 2nd Earl of Kinghorne, it is said, came 'to his inheritance the wealthiest peer in Scotland' and 'he left it the poorest'. This was largely because of his friendship with James Graham, Marquis of Montrose, with whom he joined forces. Montrose was at first a fierce Covenanter (against Popery and Episcopacy) but later became more of a Royalist. There came a point when the Earl's conscience forced him to part company with his old friend when the latter took up arms against the Covenanters, and to throw in his lot against him. He even helped finance the Covenanting army against Montrose and thus beggared himself in the process.

The 3rd Earl kept a diary which he called his 'Book of Record', the manuscript of which is in the Castle archives so we know much about him. His father died of plague when he was three and unfortunately he was mistreated by his stepfather. Leaving St Andrews at the age of 17, he went first to Castle Lyon (now Castle Huntly) where he found all the furnishings had been sold, possibly to pay his father's debts, and he even had to borrow a bed from the Minister of Longforgan. He came to Glamis with his wife in 1670 and lodged in rooms at the top of the great stair – the only part of the Castle glazed at that time.

Patrick, 9th Lord Glamis (afterwards 1st Earl of Kinghorne), succeeded to the title and property aged three. This portrait by a follower of François Clouet, shows him wearing a fashionable lace ruff collar and a jewelled hat.

On the reverse is this portrait of George Boswell his secretary, ever-ready with quill pen behind his ear!

The 2nd Earl of Kinghorne by George Jamesone. The 3rd Earl of Strathmore and Kinghorne by Jacob de Wet 1683 (detail).

He discovered the estates were burdened with debts amounting to £40,000 – an enormous sum in those days. He was advised that the situation was 'irrecoverable' but, after 40 years of determined hard work, he restored his inheritance to solvency. Patrick obtained a new charter to his patent of peerage in 1677 and was afterwards known as 'The Earl of Strathmore and Kinghorne', as have been his successors ever since.

It says much for this young man that he managed not only to pay off his debts by strict economies, but also was later able to rebuild and improve Glamis Castle to very much its appearance today. This can be seen by examining the distant view of the building in the huge family painting of him and his sons in the Drawing Room. He wrote in his diary: 'Tho' it be an old house and consequentlie was the more difficult to reduce the place to any uniformitie yet I did covet extremely to order my building so that my frontispiece might have a resemblance on both syds, and my Great Hall haveing no following was also a great inducement to me for reering up that quarter upon the west syd wch now is, so haveing first founded it, I built my walls according to my draught....'; David Scott-Moncrieff thought that this entry suggested that the Earl was his own architect.

The Earl remodelled the Castle. He added the west wing in 1679 giving a false symmetry. He swept away the courtyard buildings, laid out the main avenue at 45° to the Castle so that the large stair became the centre of the composition. In front he created a baroque setting of courts, sculptures and vistas. The interiors were equally rich. He built and decorated the Chapel. He adapted the old Great Hall of the Castle, which had already been made elegant with plasterwork in 1621, into a fine Drawing Room. He later said, 'My Great Hall, which is a room that I ever loved'. He also kept a 'private buffoon' or jester and was the last nobleman in Scotland to do so. This jester's motley is still preserved in the Castle and can be seen in the Drawing Room. There is a small copy of it which was worn by The Queen Mother's brother at a fancy dress party. It can be seen in the Family Exhibition Room. The aforementioned jester, it is recorded, was dismissed for proposing to a young lady of the house!

The 4th Earl of Strathmore married Lady Elizabeth Stanhope, a daughter of the 2nd Earl of Chesterfield. He had seven sons, two of whom became Lord Glamis, both predeceasing their father and four other brothers who succeeded to the Earldom in turn, the 8th Earl and youngest son being the only one who had an heir.

It was during the time of the 5th Earl that the family's Royalist sympathies came to the fore again when he joined the Jacobite cause and was killed at the Battle of Sheriffmuir in 1715. The following year the 6th Earl entertained the 'Old Chevalier' – James VIII and III – at Glamis together with an entourage of 88, for all of whom beds were provided. The 'Old Chevalier', as he was known, touched for the King's Evil in the Chapel. It was said that a true Sovereign could cure sufferers of this lymphatic disorder, common at the time, by touching them – faith healing we would call it today. It is said that all the sufferers who came to Glamis during the few days James stayed there were cured. This was a sure sign to Jacobites that he was the rightful King.

When the 'Old Chevalier' left the Castle, he absent-mindedly left his watch under the pillow. The maid who cleaned out the room after he had left, stole it. Many years later, a descendant of that chambermaid returned the watch to the Castle and thus to its rightful place. The watch, together with the sword which had earlier been given to the Earl, are shown in the Family Exhibition Room.

The 9th Earl was a Representative Peer for Scotland. Scottish peers did not have an automatic right to sit in the House of Lords, but had to be elected by their fellow peers to do so. In 1767 Lord Strathmore married Mary Eleanor Bowes, a great Durham heiress. She was the only daughter of Sir George Bowes of Streatlam Castle and Gibside (together with estates in Hertfordshire and elsewhere). His was a family of ancient and honourable descent – Sir Robert Bowes being Elizabeth I's Ambassador to Scotland from 1577 to 1583. With his new-found wealth the Earl remodelled much of the Castle, including the building of new kitchens and the Library wing (now Billiard Room).

John, 4th Earl by Sir Godfrey Kneller.

John, 5th Earl.

Charles, 6th Earl.

He also began remodelling the policies, removing the garden walls in front of the Castle and relocating the gates to the periphery of the policies.

The 10th Earl was also a Representative Peer, but was given the UK title of Lord Bowes, which entitled him to a seat in the Lords without election. He took the name of Bowes and later the surname Lyon was reincorporated to form the present name of Bowes Lyon. He also quartered the arms of Bowes with his own. The former were also punning arms – three bows 'proper' on an ermine background, and so the family are a great rarity in having punning arms for both their surnames on the same shield. Although he lived largely on his estates in County Durham he completed much of the work at Glamis begun by his father. He re-roofed the east wing in 1797 and rebuilt the west wing between 1798 –1801.

The 10th Earl died in 1820 the day after his marriage and he was succeeded by his brother, the 11th Earl, when the barony of Bowes became extinct. The 10th Earl had a natural son by Mary Milner. He was John Bowes who founded the Bowes Museum at Barnard Castle. The Earl married Mary Milner in an unsuccessful attempt to legitimise John Bowes. It was the 12th Earl who adopted the present family name of Bowes Lyon.

The 13th Earl modernised the Castle and made it into a comfortable home for his large family. Gas was introduced in 1865 to be replaced by electricity in 1929. He installed running water from the springs in 1865 and central heating in 1866. He built a five-acre walled garden in 1866 to provide vegetables, fruit and flowers for the Castle and in the same year re-opened the Chapel. He refaced the servants' apartments beyond the east wing in 1891–97 and in 1893 created the Dutch garden in front of the Castle.

The 20th century brought further Royal connections to Glamis with the marriage at Westminster Abbey on the 26 April 1923 between Prince Albert, Duke of York, second son of King George V, and the Lady Elizabeth Bowes Lyon, youngest daughter of the 14th Earl of Strathmore.

Claude, 13th Earl.

John 10th Earl of Strathmore by Mather Brown

The Castle c.1820 after the Baronialisation carried out by the 10th Earl of Strathmore.

Thomas, 11th Earl.

Thomas, 12th Earl.

Claude, 14th Earl.

Patrick, 15th Earl.

Timothy Patrick, 16th Earl.

This marriage was very popular in Scotland as it strengthened the ties of affection between the nation and the Royal Family which had been given such an impetus by Queen Victoria and Prince Albert. The Duke and Duchess not only shared a descent from Robert II, they were also both descended from King Henry VII, the Duchess through her mother, the Countess of Strathmore, who was a Cavendish Bentinck, the family of the Dukes of Portland.

The eldest of The Queen Mother's six brothers succeeded as 15th Earl. He served in the Scots Guards during the Great War and married a daughter of the 10th Duke of Leeds. His elder son, John, Master of Glamis, was killed in action in the Second World War whilst also serving in the Scots Guards. The 15th Earl, therefore, was succeeded by his surviving son, Timothy, who served in the Black Watch. The 16th Earl opened the Castle to visitors in 1950.

The 16th Earl died in 1972 and was succeeded by his cousin Fergus Michael Claude, 17th Earl of Strathmore and Kinghorne, son of Michael, 5th son of the 14th Earl. Educated like so many of his family at Eton, he went on to Sandhurst and became a Captain in the Scots Guards. He married Mary Pamela, the younger daughter of Brigadier N.D. McCorquodale and with his wife, he carried out extensive works to the Castle in order to make it the family home it is today. Sadly, he died in 1987 and is survived by his widow, Mary, Dowager Countess of Strathmore, their two daughters Lady Elizabeth Leeming and Lady Diana Godfrey-Faussett and was succeeded by their only son, Michael Fergus, 18th Earl of Strathmore.

The 18th Earl, Michael Fergus was educated at Sunningdale, Eton and the University of Aberdeen. He went on to The Royal Military Academy Sandhurst and then served with the Scots Guards, attaining the rank of Captain. Having qualified as a stockbroker in the City of London, he then joined the Whips Office in the House of Lords. The 18th Earl took an active role in the management of the Strathmore estates, Castle and farming enterprises and over the years made many improvements to the estate at Glamis. He cleared and restored the nineteenth century Pinetum laid out by his great great grandfather, the thirteenth Earl.

He also transformed the Walled Garden into a wonderful place for visitors, with a huge fountain, a bridge, ponds and an abundance of fruit trees, flowers and shrubs. The restoration of the Victorian bridge crossing the river dean which bears his name was another of his projects.

His voluntary roles included being President of the Boys' Brigade, Patron of The Friends of the Bowes Museum Committee and a Deputy Lieutenant for the County of Angus.

The 18th Earl married Isobel Weatherall in 1984 and had three sons Simon Patrick Lord Glamis, The Hon John Bowes Lyon and The Hon George Bowes Lyon. The marriage was dissolved in 2004. He married; secondly, Dr Damaris Stuart-William in 2005. They had one son The Hon Toby Bowes Lyon. The marriage was dissolved in 2008.

In 2012 he married Karen Rose Baxter and was a loving step-father to her daughters Chloe and Kristen. The 18th Earl died on 27th February 2016 and was succeeded by his eldest son Simon Patrick, 19th Earl of Strathmore and Kinghorne.

Born in 1986, as the eldest grandson of the 17th Earl he was styled Master of Glamis at birth. In 1987 following his Grandfather's death he became Lord Glamis, the 19th Earl of Strathmore and Kinghorne. The 19th Earl is only the third member of his family to hold all three titles.

Educated at Sunningdale school, Harrow and The Royal Agricultural University, Cirencester, he holds an M.Sc in Land Economy.

Lord Strathmore lives in Glamis Castle and takes an active role in the management of his estates both here at Glamis and at Holwick in County Durham.

Fergus, 17th Earl.

Michael Fergus, 18th Earl.

Simon, 19th Earl.

GLORIOUS GLAMIS EVENTS, ATTRACTIONS AND SPECTACLES

The Pavilion Shop has a range of unique Glamis Castle products, including crystal and bone china pieces. Reproductions of pieces in the Castle, fine woollens and tartans, hand-made lace, crafts and fashion accessories are also available. In the Food Shop you can buy local produce, honey, shortbread and Glamis' own-brand beers as well as light refreshments. For heartier meals, the Victorian Kitchen Restaurant can supply hot or cold meals and children's lunch packs.

There is a an array of events throughout the season, from spectacular outdoor concerts, the annual Strathmore Highland Games is not to be missed, and of course, The Strathmore Vintage Vehicle Extravaganza.

For more information, why not visit our website: www.glamis-castle.co.uk or please call the office on 01307 840393, send an email to: enquiries@glamis-castle.co.uk or drop by in person.

Artworked by Robertson Printers, Forfar.

The Editor and Publishers are grateful to the many previous contributors
to guidebooks of Glamis Castle; especially Robert Innes-Smith and Christopher Dingwall.
Photographs primarily by Nick McCann and Peter Smith.
Other photographers' work has been credited individually.

Produced & published by Strathmore Estates
The Estates Office, Glamis, Angus DD8 1RJ.
Email: enquiries@glamis-castle.co.uk
www.glamis-castle.co.uk
© Strathmore Estates 2018

Printed and bound by Robertson Printers, Forfar.